CHOCO ODY

The Transgender Baddie

Copyright © 2025 by Choco Ody

All rights reserved. No part of this publication may be reproduced, stored or transmitted in any form or by any means, electronic, mechanical, photocopying, recording, scanning, or otherwise without written permission from the publisher. It is illegal to copy this book, post it to a website, or distribute it by any other means without permission.

First edition

*This book was professionally typeset on Reedsy.
Find out more at reedsy.com*

Dedicated to all book lovers

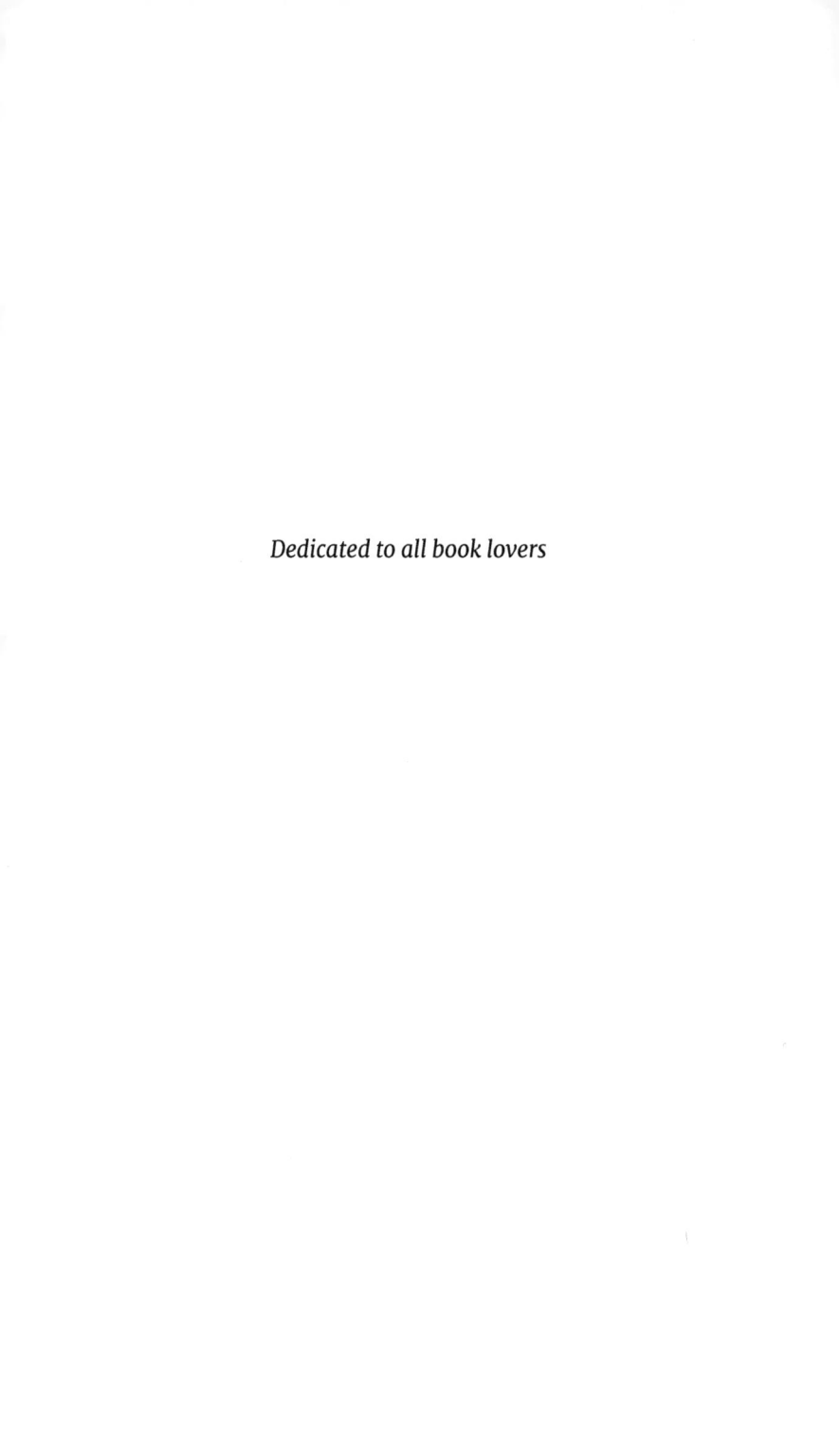

Contents

Preface   ii
Acknowledgments   iv

I   Part One

1	Chapter 1	3
2	Chapter 2	8
3	Chapter 3	14
4	Chapter 4	20
5	Chapter 5	27
6	Chapter 6	33
7	Chapter 7	38
8	Chapter 8	44
9	Chapter 9	50
10	Chapter 10	56

Preface

The Transgender Baddie is a compelling and inspiring tale that follows the journey of Titi, a transgender woman who embarks on a transformative path to not only discover her own voice but to create a platform that amplifies the stories and struggles of the transgender community. Set in a world where trans voices are often silenced or marginalized, Titi's story is one of resilience, empowerment, and hope.

The book chronicles Titi's early days of self-discovery, her partnership with her best friend Chika, and the challenges they face in building a digital platform aimed at empowering transgender people. As the platform grows, so does the impact it has on individuals from all walks of life, helping them find community, acceptance, and validation. Along the way, Titi navigates personal struggles, societal prejudices, and moments of self-doubt, but with each challenge, she grows stronger and more determined.

Through Titi's journey, the reader is introduced to the powerful bonds of friendship, the strength of transgender people, and the importance of creating spaces where individuals can be their authentic selves. The platform becomes more than just a business venture; it becomes a lifeline for many, offering solace, support, and the opportunity to be seen. Titi's success isn't just her own—it's a collective victory for the entire transgender community.

At its core, The Transgender Baddie is about finding purpose, fighting for justice, and standing proudly in one's truth. It's a story about building something meaningful from the ground up and using one's platform to create real change. Ultimately, it's about the journey of transformation—both personal and societal—and the belief that one person, with love and determination, can change the world.

Acknowledgments

Thanks for the love and support.

I

Part One

1

Chapter 1

As dawn broke over the city, the streets of Lagos came alive, bustling with the usual chaos of traffic, street vendors, and the hum of daily life. But amidst the ordinary hustle, something extraordinary was unfolding. Titi had been waiting for this moment her entire life.

She stood in front of her bathroom mirror, looking at her reflection with a mixture of excitement and trepidation. Her hair, now long and flowing in a cascade of dark curls, framed her face perfectly. Her skin had that glowing radiance that came with newfound confidence. She had never felt more herself, more whole. Today, she was finally going to embrace the woman she had always known herself to be, fully and without apology.

The journey to this moment had been a long one, filled with twists, turns, and a great deal of inner turmoil. Titi had always known she wasn't like the other boys. Growing up in a tight-knit Nigerian community, where traditions ran deep and the expectations of society were often stifling, Titi's true self had been locked away for many years. She had always felt like she was playing a role, pretending to be someone she wasn't, trying to fit into a mold that didn't quite match her true essence.

But now, after years of struggle and self-discovery, Titi was ready to take the leap. The day had come to stop hiding and to live her truth. It was a moment of courage—a bold step toward the future she had long dreamed of.

As she applied a touch of makeup to accentuate her features, she thought about the path that had led her here. Growing up, Titi had always been the odd one out in her family. Her parents, devout and traditional, had wanted a son, someone who could carry on the family name and uphold the values of their culture. Instead, they had a child who, from an early age, expressed a desire to be something else, something beyond the expectations that were set for her. Titi had always been drawn to things that were considered "feminine" by the world's standards—playing with dolls, wearing dresses, and developing a love for the finer details of life. Yet, no matter how much she expressed these desires, she was often met with confusion and resistance.

Her father had been especially difficult to deal with, always trying to suppress her individuality. He would say things like, "Boys don't wear pink," or "A man doesn't cry." Titi, too young to understand the complexities of gender identity, thought that maybe there was something wrong with her. She tried, with every fiber of her being, to conform to the expectations placed on her, but nothing ever felt right. Every time she looked in the mirror, she saw a stranger—a boy she couldn't recognize.

CHAPTER 1

It wasn't until her teenage years that she started to make sense of her feelings. She found solace in the stories of transgender people, reading books and articles about others who had gone through similar experiences. She began to understand that what she had felt all her life wasn't a curse or something to be ashamed of—it was who she truly was. She was a woman, and nothing could change that.

But knowing who she was inside and outside were two different things. Titi had struggled with her appearance, constantly trying to fit into the body she was born with, but finding no comfort in it. Every inch of her felt like an alien landscape, a reminder that she was trapped in someone else's idea of who she should be. The more she tried to suppress her femininity, the more it screamed for expression.

At first, the thought of transitioning seemed impossible. The cost, the risk, the fear of rejection from her family and society—it all felt like too much to bear. But there was something deep inside her that urged her to go forward. Titi had always been the type of person who believed in taking bold risks, even when the odds were stacked against her. She wasn't going to let fear control her life any longer. So, she saved up money, did her research, and started seeing a doctor who specialized in gender affirming care.

The process had been slow, but it had been worth it. Every step brought her closer to the woman she had always known she was meant to be. Hormone therapy had softened her features, and little by little, she felt her body aligning with her spirit. There were moments of doubt, especially when she faced the judgmental stares of strangers or the cold silence from her family. But there were also moments of pure joy—when she wore her first dress, when she finally saw her reflection and smiled, knowing it was truly her staring back.

Today was a big day for Titi. She was about to attend a party—one that was being thrown by a friend who had been supportive throughout her transition. It wasn't just any party, though. This was a celebration of all the people in the transgender community who had fought, struggled, and triumphed in their journeys. Titi had always felt like an outsider in the world, but tonight, she would be surrounded by people who understood her, who knew exactly what it was like to face adversity and still rise above it.

She slipped into her dress, a beautiful red number that hugged her curves in all the right ways. She had spent hours picking it out, wanting to make a statement without saying a word. The dress made her feel powerful, sexy, and confident. She applied a touch of perfume, adjusted her earrings, and stepped back to admire herself.

The reflection staring back at her now was not the same one she had seen years ago. This version of Titi was unapologetically herself. She had made it. She had overcome the barriers that society had placed in her way, the restrictions of culture and tradition, and now she was free. She was the transgender baddie.

As she stepped out of her apartment and into the Lagos night, Titi felt an overwhelming sense of peace. She was no longer hiding in the shadows, pretending to be someone she wasn't. She was a woman, a queen, and nothing could take that away

CHAPTER 1

from her.

The road to get here had been difficult, but as she walked through the vibrant streets of Lagos, she felt an undeniable sense of freedom. She was ready to conquer whatever came next. No longer a prisoner to her past, Titi was stepping boldly into her future, ready to live her truth and be unapologetically herself. Tonight was just the beginning.

As she arrived at the party, the atmosphere was electric. Laughter and music filled the air, and people embraced one another, sharing stories of their triumphs and struggles. Titi felt like she had finally found her tribe. For the first time in her life, she wasn't alone in her journey.

The night was filled with laughter, dancing, and celebration. Titi moved through the crowd, making new friends, reconnecting with old ones, and feeling a sense of belonging she had never experienced before. It was the night of her life—a night of acceptance, love, and joy.

Titi wasn't just surviving anymore. She was thriving.

Chapter 2

The morning after the party, Titi woke up to the gentle warmth of the Lagos sun filtering through the windows of her small apartment. The echoes of laughter and music from the night before still reverberated in her mind, and a soft smile tugged at her lips. She felt a deep sense of contentment, like a piece of herself had finally found its rightful place in the world. Last night had been an unforgettable moment—one that marked not just a celebration of her journey, but a confirmation that she belonged.

Sitting up in bed, Titi stretched and glanced at the clock on her nightstand. It was a Saturday, and she had the whole day ahead of her. There was no work to rush off to, no appointments to make, no one to answer to except herself. She could finally breathe easy, free from the pressures that had weighed her down for so many years.

But as the initial wave of peace washed over her, it was quickly followed by a familiar knot in her stomach. Her parents. The

CHAPTER 2

thought of them always brought a lingering sadness, a reminder of the chasm that had grown between them since she began her transition. Despite the strides she had made in her own personal life, the relationship with her family remained strained, an unspoken tension hanging in the air every time they spoke.

It had been months since the last time she had seen them. Her mother had called on her birthday, offering a curt "Happy birthday, my son," a line that still stung. Her father's silence had been even more deafening. Titi had reached out to them several times, hoping for a breakthrough, a sign that they would come to accept her for who she truly was. But each time, the response was distant, cold, as if they were struggling to reconcile the daughter they knew with the woman she had become.

Titi had made peace with the fact that it would take time—time for them to understand, time for them to adjust. She had to live her life for herself now. But that didn't make it any easier. The longing for their acceptance, their love, was a constant ache in her heart.

Sighing, she swung her legs over the side of the bed and stood up, stretching again to shake off the lingering sadness. There was no point dwelling on what she couldn't change. She had worked too hard to get here, too hard to let her family's rejection pull her back into a place of doubt. She had come so far, and she knew that her journey wasn't just about finding herself—it was about redefining what happiness meant on her own terms.

Titi wandered into the kitchen and started brewing a cup of coffee. The rich aroma filled the small space, grounding her in the present moment. She had learned to appreciate these quiet mornings, the simplicity of life. It was in these moments that she could truly be herself, without the masks or expectations of others.

The faint sound of her phone vibrating on the counter interrupted her thoughts. She reached for it, half-expecting it to be a message from her best friend, Chika, who had been her rock throughout the entire transition. Chika was one of the few people who had always been there for her—understanding, accepting, and never once questioning her decision to live as her authentic self.

Sure enough, the message was from Chika.

"Hey sis, I was thinking we could go to the beach today. Just chill, catch up, you know. What do you think?"

Titi smiled as she read the message. It was exactly what she needed. A day of relaxation, free from the complications of life. She quickly typed a reply.

"Sounds perfect! I'll be ready in an hour."

As she sipped her coffee, Titi thought about the importance of the people who had supported her. It was one thing to come out to the world, but it was another to have people who truly saw her, who didn't just tolerate her but embraced her. Chika had been one of the first to call her out on her potential, to remind her that she was a force to be reckoned with. That encouragement had pushed Titi to pursue her dreams, to take bold risks, and to

CHAPTER 2

never look back.

An hour later, Titi met Chika at the beach, the salty air and crashing waves greeting them with a sense of calm. The sun was already high in the sky, warming the golden sand beneath their feet. It was the perfect day for a getaway—just the two of them, away from the hustle and bustle of the city.

The two women settled under a large umbrella, setting up their beach towels and soaking in the sun. Chika handed Titi a cold drink, and the two of them chatted effortlessly, catching up on everything from work to relationships, from family to new projects. It was refreshing to be with someone who didn't treat her as a project or a cause to be understood. With Chika, she was just Titi—uncomplicated and free.

As they talked, a group of people walked by, casting curious glances at the two women. Titi noticed it immediately—the subtle way they looked at her, as if she were somehow out of place. She had grown used to these moments, to the whispers and the stares, but today it stung just a little more. She could feel the weight of their judgment on her shoulders, a silent reminder that the world was still catching up to the idea of what it meant to be a transgender woman in Lagos.

Chika, ever the observant friend, noticed the change in Titi's demeanor. She leaned over, placing a hand on her shoulder.

"Don't let them bother you, Titi," Chika said softly. "You've come so far. You're a queen, and you deserve to take up space in this world. Don't let anyone make you feel small."

Titi's eyes softened at Chika's words. She had always been her biggest cheerleader, and for that, Titi was forever grateful.

"I know," Titi replied, her voice steady but with a hint of vulnerability. "It's just... sometimes I wonder if the world will ever accept me, truly accept me. Or if I'll always have to fight for my place."

Chika nodded, her expression understanding. "The world isn't always kind, especially when it comes to things it doesn't understand. But you know what? You're not fighting alone. You have people who love you, who see you for who you are, and who will always stand by your side. And trust me, as time goes on, more and more people will realize that you don't have to fit into a box. You're Titi, and that's enough."

Titi smiled, feeling a warmth spread through her chest. Chika was right. She didn't need anyone's validation but her own. She had come this far by trusting herself, by following her heart. And she knew that, no matter what, she would continue to forge her own path.

The afternoon slipped by lazily as the two friends relaxed on the beach. Titi felt the weight of the world lift off her shoulders, if only for a moment. As the sun began to set, painting the sky with hues of pink and orange, she knew that she was on the right path. No matter the challenges ahead, she had found peace within herself, and that was more than enough.

When the day came to an end, Titi felt a renewed sense of purpose. The road ahead was still uncertain, but one thing was clear—she was ready to face whatever came her way. She was no longer just surviving. She was living, truly living, and she was going to keep going until the world saw her, not as a label or a stereotype, but as Titi—the woman who had the courage to live her truth.

Chapter 3

The week after their beach outing, Titi found herself walking down a street she knew all too well. It was a quiet Friday afternoon, the kind of day when the city felt almost deserted— no traffic jams, no honking horns, just the faint hum of life happening in the background. She was on her way to an important meeting, one that could determine the next big step in her career. But as she walked, her mind kept wandering to thoughts of the past and the struggle to reconcile her old life with the person she had become.

A few years ago, this street would have felt like home—she had spent so many hours in these very shops and cafes, exchanging pleasantries with familiar faces. But now, it felt different. It was a reminder of who she used to be, and more importantly, of the people she had left behind. It wasn't just her family that she had distanced herself from. There were friends, acquaintances— people who had once been a part of her world but who had slowly faded as she stepped into the woman she was always meant to be.

CHAPTER 3

Her phone buzzed in her bag, breaking her from her thoughts. She reached for it and smiled when she saw the message was from Chika.

"You good? Ready for the meeting?"

Titi typed a quick reply. *"Yes, just a little nervous. But I'm ready."*

Chika's response was almost immediate. *"You've got this! I know you do. Just remember, you've worked hard to get here. No one can take that from you."*

Titi tucked her phone back into her bag and took a deep breath. It was just another hurdle, another step toward living her truth. She had faced rejection before—disappointment, prejudice, the occasional moments of doubt. But every time, she had come out stronger. She was no longer the person she once was. No longer the quiet, unsure individual who lived in fear of being discovered. She was Titi. She was bold. She was unapologetically herself.

The meeting was at one of the city's most prestigious advertising firms. Titi had been given the opportunity to pitch her concept for a new campaign aimed at empowering marginalized voices, specifically those of the LGBTQ+ community. It was a project she was passionate about, a chance to use her platform to highlight the issues that affected people like her. As she walked into the building, the familiar buzz of anticipation filled her chest. She had spent weeks preparing for this moment, and now, it was finally time to see it through.

The receptionist greeted her with a friendly smile and directed her to the conference room. The large glass walls offered a panoramic view of the city, the skyline stretching out in every direction. It was a stunning sight, but Titi's focus was on the task at hand. She had come here to make her mark. Nothing else mattered.

The moment she stepped into the conference room, the energy shifted. The room was filled with a group of people, all seated around a long wooden table. Some of them looked up with mild curiosity, while others were already engaged in their own conversations. Titi took a seat at the head of the table, trying her best to remain composed despite the nerves that gnawed at her.

One of the senior executives, a middle-aged man with a polished suit and glasses, greeted her with a nod. "Titi, it's great to finally meet you in person. We've heard a lot of good things about you."

"Thank you for having me," she replied, keeping her voice steady. She cleared her throat and set her laptop in front of her, ready to begin her presentation.

The pitch started off smoothly. She introduced the concept, speaking about the importance of representation and how the campaign would highlight the stories of people from diverse backgrounds. She spoke with passion, every word carefully chosen to convey the message she believed in. As she spoke, she could feel the room's attention shifting, their eyes no longer distant but focused on her.

CHAPTER 3

As she began outlining the specifics of the campaign—social media strategies, partnerships, and the overall aesthetic—she noticed a few skeptical glances exchanged between some of the executives. She had seen this before, the doubt, the questioning. She knew what it meant. It wasn't her idea they were questioning. It was her. Her identity, her authenticity.

One of the executives, a woman in her early thirties, spoke up. "This is an interesting concept, but I have to admit, I'm concerned about how the audience will respond to such a bold campaign. Do you think there will be pushback? People can be very resistant to change, especially when it comes to sensitive topics like gender identity."

Titi paused for a moment, her gaze steady. She had been anticipating this question. "I understand your concern," she said carefully. "But it's important to recognize that the world is changing. People are beginning to understand the value of inclusivity and representation. And yes, there may be some resistance—but that's exactly why this campaign is necessary. It's time to give these voices a platform."

The room was quiet for a moment, the weight of her words hanging in the air. Titi could feel her heart racing, but she refused to let the nerves take over. This was her time to prove that her perspective mattered. That she mattered.

Another executive, a man in his forties with salt-and-pepper hair, leaned forward. "I see your point, Titi. But how do you plan to ensure that the campaign feels authentic? There are plenty of initiatives out there that claim to support marginalized groups, but sometimes they end up feeling tokenistic. How can we avoid that?"

Titi nodded, acknowledging the valid concern. "Authenticity is key. This campaign isn't about checking a box or satisfying a trend. It's about sharing real stories, lifting up voices that have long been silenced. We'll be working with people from the community, ensuring that their stories are told by those who know the truth, not just by outsiders trying to profit from their experiences."

The discussion continued for another hour, with Titi answering each question with poise and conviction. Despite the tension in the room, she could sense that her message was starting to resonate. By the time she finished her presentation, the executives seemed much more engaged, nodding and taking notes as she concluded.

"Thank you for your time," Titi said, standing up and packing away her materials. "I believe in this project, and I believe in the power of storytelling to bring about change."

The senior executive who had greeted her earlier stood up as well, extending a hand. "Titi, thank you. This has been a very insightful presentation. We'll be in touch soon."

Titi smiled, shaking his hand. "I look forward to hearing from you."

As she left the building, a sense of relief washed over her. The meeting had gone better than she expected. But more than that, she felt proud of herself. For the first time in a long while, she felt like she was truly walking in her purpose. This campaign wasn't just a job—it was a chance to make a real difference, to show the world that trans voices were not just worthy of being heard, but were integral to the conversation about representation and equality.

As she made her way back to her car, her phone buzzed again. This time, it was a text from her mother. Her heart skipped a beat as she saw the message.

"I've been thinking about you. We need to talk."

Titi's breath caught in her throat. Her heart raced, but this time, it wasn't from nerves. It was a mix of excitement and fear. Could this be the breakthrough she had been waiting for? Could this be the first step toward healing the rift that had existed between them for so long?

She didn't know what the conversation would bring, but she knew one thing for sure—she was ready. She was ready to confront the past, to rebuild what had been broken, and to show her family that she was no longer afraid to be the woman she had always been. No matter what happened next, she was no longer running from herself.

She hit reply on her phone. *"I'd like that, Mom. Let's talk."*

The road ahead was uncertain, but for the first time in a long while, Titi felt a sense of hope. A sense of possibility. And that, in itself, was enough to carry her forward.

Chapter 4

Titi sat at her kitchen table, the steaming cup of tea in front of her, its warmth a small comfort as she stared at the phone in her hand. Her mother's message had been haunting her all week. *"We need to talk."* It was simple, yet it carried so much weight. For years, there had been an unspoken tension between them. A rift that neither of them seemed capable of bridging. And now, her mother wanted to talk. Titi knew this conversation could change everything.

Her mind raced with questions, most of which she knew she couldn't answer. What would her mother say? Was she ready for this? Was her mother ready for this? For all the self-assurance Titi had built up in her career and her personal life, this one relationship still had the power to shake her to her core. After all, it wasn't just a mother and daughter relationship; it was also the relationship between a woman who had chosen to live her truth and a mother who had struggled with the reality of that truth.

CHAPTER 4

The clock on the wall ticked away as she absentmindedly stared at her phone. Every time she thought about texting her mother to set up a time to talk, her nerves overtook her. She wanted to be strong, but the thought of confronting the past and all its unresolved emotions made her feel vulnerable. For years, she had lived with the expectation that one day she would have to confront her mother's rejection and disapproval. Yet, she had always hoped that day would never come. Now, it seemed inevitable.

The doorbell rang, pulling her out of her thoughts. Titi took a deep breath and stood up. Her heels clicked against the polished wood floor as she walked toward the door. She wasn't expecting anyone, but when she opened it, she found Chika standing on the other side with a big smile plastered across her face.

"Hey, sis! What's going on?" Chika's energy was as infectious as ever. Titi couldn't help but smile in return, though it was a smile tinged with uncertainty.

"Not much. Just... thinking," Titi replied, stepping aside to let Chika in.

Chika raised an eyebrow. "Thinking? About what? You're not still stressing about that meeting, are you? You nailed it, Titi. You were on fire!"

Titi chuckled softly. "No, it's not the meeting. It's... my mom. She texted me this week. She said we need to talk."

Chika's face softened instantly. "Oh, I see. That's... big. Have you set a time to talk?"

Titi shook her head. "I haven't. I've been putting it off. I'm not sure I'm ready for whatever she wants to say."

Chika nodded, understanding. "I get it. It's never easy dealing with family stuff, especially when it's something that's been hanging over your head for so long. But you can't avoid it forever, Titi. You have to face it."

"I know. But I'm scared, Chika. What if she doesn't accept me? What if she can't understand who I am?" Titi's voice trembled slightly, and she felt the familiar sting of fear rising in her chest.

Chika placed a reassuring hand on her shoulder. "You're stronger than you think. And you know what? If anyone can understand you, it's your mom. She's the one who raised you, the one who taught you how to be the amazing person you are. Yeah, it's going to be tough, but I believe she'll come around. And if not... well, we're your family too. You've got people who love you no matter what."

Titi took a deep breath, absorbing Chika's words. Her friend's unwavering support was a balm to her anxious soul. Chika had been there for her in ways no one else had. She had watched her navigate the challenges of transitioning, and she had always stood by her side, even when Titi didn't feel like she deserved it. She owed it to herself—and to her mom—to at least have this conversation.

"I know you're right," Titi said finally, her voice steadier than

CHAPTER 4

before. "I just... I need to be ready for whatever happens."

Chika smiled warmly. "Of course. And when you're ready, we'll all be here for you. Just know that you don't have to face this alone."

Titi hugged her friend tightly. "Thank you, Chika. I don't know what I'd do without you."

Chika squeezed her back and then pulled away. "I'm going to make you a strong cup of coffee, and we're going to figure this out, okay?"

"Okay," Titi replied, feeling a sense of peace settle over her.

As Chika moved to the kitchen, Titi returned to her phone. This time, she took a deep breath and typed out a simple message to her mother.

"Mom, I think we should talk too. When would be a good time for you?"

She hit send and waited. The response didn't come right away, but when it did, it was exactly what Titi had hoped for.

"How about Sunday afternoon? I've missed you, Titi."

Titi's heart fluttered at the words. For the first time in years, she felt a small spark of hope. Maybe this conversation could be the beginning of something new, something healing.

The weekend passed in a blur. Titi found herself lost in a whirlwind of nerves and anticipation. She went through her usual routine—working on her latest campaign, meeting with clients, and responding to emails—but her thoughts kept drifting back to her mother. What would this conversation look like? How would it unfold? She tried not to overthink it, but she couldn't help herself.

Finally, Sunday afternoon arrived. Titi had spent the morning pacing around her apartment, trying to calm herself. She wasn't sure what she expected, but she knew she had to be prepared for anything. She had dressed carefully for the occasion, opting for a simple yet elegant outfit—something that made her feel confident but not overly flashy.

When the doorbell rang, her heart nearly stopped. She took a deep breath and opened the door. There stood her mother, looking as elegant as ever. Titi could see the signs of age in her face—more wrinkles, a touch of gray in her hair—but there was no mistaking the love and concern in her eyes.

"Titi..." Her mother's voice trembled slightly, as though she wasn't sure what to say next.

"Hi, Mom." Titi's voice was soft but steady. She stepped aside to let her mother into the apartment, feeling the weight of the moment settle around them.

They stood in silence for a moment, both unsure of where to start. Finally, Titi spoke. "I'm glad you reached out. I've been thinking about this a lot."

CHAPTER 4

Her mother nodded. "I know. I've been thinking too. About everything... about you."

Titi's heart skipped a beat. This was it. The moment she had feared and longed for all at once.

"I'm sorry, Titi," her mother continued, her voice cracking. "I'm sorry for all the years I didn't understand. For not being there when you needed me most."

Titi's breath caught in her throat. She had been prepared for rejection, for anger, but not for this. Not for an apology.

"I didn't know how to accept it," her mother said softly. "I didn't know how to accept you. But I see now... I see how strong you are. How beautiful you are, inside and out. And I'm sorry for not seeing that sooner."

Titi felt tears welling up in her eyes, but she fought them back. She had never imagined this moment would come—at least, not like this. For so long, she had carried the weight of her mother's disapproval, the feeling of being unworthy of her love. But now, as she looked at her mother, she saw something else. She saw vulnerability, regret, and most importantly, a willingness to change.

"I love you, Titi," her mother whispered, stepping forward to take her hand. "I may not understand everything, but I love you. And I want to be part of your life. I want to be there for you."

Titi's heart swelled with emotion. This was the conversation she had been waiting for, the one that could finally heal the wounds that had festered for years. And in that moment, surrounded by the woman who had given her life, Titi knew that the road ahead wouldn't be easy, but it would be worth it.

Together, they would rebuild their bond. Together, they would move forward.

Chapter 5

The bright city lights of Lagos flickered through the window as Titi sat at her desk, her laptop open in front of her. It was a typical Friday evening, yet tonight felt different. There was a heaviness in the air, a feeling that lingered in her chest, one that she couldn't shake off. The conversation with her mother had gone better than she had ever imagined. The warmth of her mother's acceptance still hung in the air, but there was something else too. A feeling of uncertainty, as though the road ahead was uncharted, and she wasn't sure where it would lead.

She ran a hand through her hair and leaned back in her chair. The city buzzed outside, its constant hum a backdrop to her own inner turbulence. Her career was thriving, her relationships were strong, and yet, there was this underlying fear of what the future held. She couldn't help but wonder: would she always feel this way? Would the weight of being different, of standing out, always weigh on her?

A soft knock on the door broke her reverie. Titi looked up to see

Chika standing in the doorway, her usual bright smile lighting up the room. "Hey, I brought food," she said, holding up a bag of takeout.

Titi smiled in return, grateful for the distraction. "You're a lifesaver," she said, standing up to meet her friend.

Chika walked in, setting the bag down on the table. "You've been working all day, haven't you? You need a break."

"I'm fine," Titi replied, trying to sound more upbeat than she felt. "It's just... a lot on my mind."

Chika gave her a knowing look as she pulled out containers of jollof rice and fried plantains. "I know that look. Spill. What's going on?"

Titi hesitated for a moment, her gaze drifting to the window. "I guess I'm just... unsure. About everything. The conversation with my mom, it went well, but I feel like there's so much more to unpack. I've spent so many years hiding who I am, trying to fit into a mold that wasn't me, and now that things are finally starting to change, I'm scared. Scared of losing everything, scared of the unknown."

Chika set down the food and sat across from Titi, her expression softening. "I get it. You've been through a lot, and it's not going to change overnight. But the fact that your mom is finally accepting you, that's huge. You've got this, Titi. You've always had this."

CHAPTER 5

Titi sighed, rubbing her temples. "I don't know. There's still this part of me that feels like I'm living on borrowed time, like one wrong move and everything will crumble."

"You're stronger than you give yourself credit for," Chika said gently. "And no one is perfect, Titi. Not even your mom. But you're here. You're living your truth, and that's something to be proud of."

Titi looked at her friend, the sincerity in her eyes helping to ground her. "Thanks, Chika. I don't say it enough, but you've been a constant in my life. You've been here for me, even when I didn't deserve it."

Chika waved her hand dismissively. "Please, stop. You don't have to thank me. That's what friends are for. Besides, you've always been there for me, even when life got tough."

Titi smiled, feeling a sense of warmth spread through her chest. As much as she tried to convince herself she didn't need anyone, the truth was, Chika was right. She couldn't do this alone. She never had to.

The two women spent the next few hours talking, laughing, and eating. For a moment, Titi allowed herself to forget about the pressures and uncertainties that had been consuming her. She let herself enjoy the simple comfort of good food and great company. The laughter they shared was genuine, and in that moment, it was as if all the world's problems had faded into the background.

But as the night wore on, Titi's thoughts inevitably drifted back to the conversation with her mother. She had left their meeting with a sense of hope, but the reality of it all was still settling in. What would their relationship look like now? Could things truly change, or was it too late for them to rebuild?

The sound of her phone vibrating on the table broke her thoughts. She picked it up, expecting a work-related message, but instead, it was a text from her mother.

"I've been thinking about you all day. I'm so proud of you, Titi. I'm here whenever you need me."

Titi felt a lump form in her throat as she read the words. It was one thing to hear those words in person, but to read them in writing, coming from the woman who had been so distant for so long, it hit her harder than she expected.

Chika noticed the change in her expression and leaned over. "What's up?"

Titi showed her the text, and Chika smiled. "See? She's trying, Titi. She's really trying."

"I know," Titi replied softly, her voice catching. "It's just... I've been carrying this weight for so long, Chika. I don't know how to let go of it."

Chika placed a hand on her shoulder. "You don't have to let go all at once. It's a process. But you'll get there. Just take it one step at a time."

CHAPTER 5

Titi nodded, her mind swirling with emotions. She wanted to believe that things could get better, that she could finally heal the wounds that had been left open for so long. But a part of her remained cautious. The fear of being hurt again, of being rejected again, was still very real.

That night, as Chika left and the apartment settled into silence, Titi found herself staring at the stars outside her window. The city below was alive with activity, but she felt oddly isolated, as though she were standing on the edge of something, unsure of what lay beyond.

Her thoughts drifted back to the childhood memories of her mother. She remembered the moments when they had been close, before everything had changed. She remembered her mother's laughter, her gentle touch, the way she had always tried to protect her. But then the tension had started to build, the silent disapproval, the unspoken words that had turned everything cold.

Titi had always felt that disconnect, that sense that something was missing, but she had never been able to put her finger on it. And now, years later, it seemed as though her mother was trying to bridge that gap. But would it be enough? Would her mother truly accept her, flaws and all?

As the night wore on, Titi found herself reflecting on the woman she had become. She had fought for her place in the world, for the right to be who she was, and now, she was fighting for her relationship with her mother. She knew it wouldn't be easy, but she also knew that it was worth it. Her mother was trying, and for the first time in a long while, Titi felt a glimmer of hope.

She had come so far, and though the road ahead was uncertain, she was ready to take the next step. With Chika by her side and her mother's tentative support, she felt stronger than she ever had before. The future was still a mystery, but one thing was clear: Titi was no longer afraid to face it.

As the city lights continued to flicker below, Titi made a silent promise to herself: no matter what happened, she would keep moving forward. She had found her truth, and nothing could take that away from her.

Chapter 6

The air felt different that morning. Titi woke up to the sound of birds chirping outside her window, their melodic songs filtering through the slight crack she had left open. It was a Saturday, and for once, she didn't have a million things on her to-do list. She was still in the midst of figuring out what her next steps would be, but for the first time in a long while, she felt calm.

She stretched, slowly rising from her bed as the warmth of the early morning sun bathed the room. Her apartment, a modest but cozy space in the heart of Lagos, had become a sanctuary for her. It was where she could reflect on her journey, where she could breathe and let her mind wander without the pressures of the outside world. But today, something felt different.

Titi stood in front of her mirror, staring at her reflection. She had come a long way, and while the road ahead was still uncertain, she had a sense of peace that had eluded her for much of her life. The conversation with her mother had been transformative. Her mother had finally seen her, truly seen her for who she was, and

Titi had finally stopped running from herself.

The doorbell rang, breaking her trance. She walked over to the door and opened it to find Chika standing there, her usual bright smile in place.

"Morning, superstar," Chika said, holding up a bag of pastries. "I thought we could have breakfast together. It's been too long since we've done this."

Titi smiled, grateful for her friend's consistent presence. "Come in, Chika. You didn't have to bring food, but I'm not complaining."

Chika walked in, setting the bag down on the kitchen counter. "Well, I figured if we were going to talk, we might as well have something good to eat, right?"

Titi chuckled, shaking her head as she sat down at the kitchen table. "You're right. I've been so caught up in everything lately that I haven't even had time to just relax."

Chika pulled out the pastries, and the two women sat together, chatting about everything and nothing. For a few moments, Titi allowed herself to forget about the weight of the world outside. It was easy to get caught up in the big questions: What did the future hold? Would her mother's acceptance truly last? What did it mean to be truly free? But today, she just needed to breathe.

"So," Chika began after a while, her voice turning more serious. "How are you really doing? I mean, we talk a lot, but I know

CHAPTER 6

there's a lot more going on in that head of yours."

Titi took a deep breath, setting her pastry down. She appreciated Chika's bluntness. It was part of what made their friendship so real. "I'm... okay," she said slowly. "I guess I've just been processing everything. The conversation with my mom... it went well, better than I could have hoped for, but there's still this part of me that's scared. Scared of what comes next."

Chika nodded, her eyes soft with understanding. "You're allowed to feel that way, Titi. You've spent so many years holding everything in, building up walls to protect yourself. It's going to take time to let those walls come down."

Titi looked down at her hands, fidgeting with her fingers. "I know. But what if things change again? What if I lose this, lose the only thing I've ever wanted: my mother's acceptance?"

"You won't lose it," Chika replied firmly. "She's your mother. She might not have understood you at first, but she's trying now. That's more than a lot of people get."

Titi sighed, her mind still clouded with uncertainty. "It's just hard to trust that things will stay this way. I spent so many years hiding, and now that I'm finally being true to myself, it feels like I'm walking on eggshells. I don't know what's safe anymore."

Chika placed a hand on hers, offering a steadying presence. "You've got to trust yourself, Titi. You've come this far. You're not going to undo all your progress just because it's hard. You're stronger than you give yourself credit for."

Titi looked up at her friend, a small smile tugging at the corner of her lips. "Thanks, Chika. I really needed to hear that."

They sat in silence for a moment, the weight of their conversation settling in. There was so much that Titi still needed to process, but she knew she didn't have to do it alone. She had Chika, and for the first time in a long time, she had her mother's tentative support.

As the morning wore on, Titi found herself reflecting on the path that had brought her here. It hadn't been an easy journey, but it had been worth it. Every struggle, every setback, had led her to this moment of clarity. She was no longer hiding, no longer apologizing for who she was. And that, she realized, was the greatest gift she could give herself.

Later that afternoon, Titi found herself sitting in the park, the cool breeze rustling the leaves of the trees around her. She watched as people walked by, lost in their own worlds, and for a moment, she felt completely at peace. It wasn't often that she allowed herself these moments of stillness, but today, she needed it.

Her phone buzzed in her pocket, pulling her from her thoughts. She pulled it out and saw that it was a message from her mom. *"I was thinking about you today. I hope you're doing okay. You know I'm always here for you, right?"*

Titi felt her heart skip a beat as she read the words. It was a simple message, but it carried so much weight. For years, she had longed for her mother's approval, and now that it was finally

CHAPTER 6

within her reach, she felt an overwhelming mix of emotions.

She typed a quick reply. *"I'm doing well. Thank you for reaching out. It means more to me than I can express."*

She hit send, then stared at the screen for a moment before setting the phone down. She wasn't sure where things would go from here, but for the first time, she wasn't afraid. She had taken the first step toward healing, toward mending the relationship with her mother, and she was proud of that.

As the sun began to set, casting a golden glow over the park, Titi smiled to herself. It was a small moment, but it was enough. She had come so far, and though the road ahead was still uncertain, she knew she wasn't walking it alone. The future was hers to shape, and for the first time, she was ready to face it head-on.

She took a deep breath, feeling the cool air fill her lungs. Whatever came next, she would be ready.

Chapter 7

The early morning mist had started to dissipate, giving way to a bright, unrelenting sun. Titi stood by her window, watching the world wake up. The streets of Lagos had already started to come to life, with cars honking, people shouting, and the usual bustle of the city surrounding her apartment building. It felt like the city never slept, constantly moving, constantly changing. Titi felt like she had been in motion her whole life, always adjusting, always evolving. But now, something felt different.

She felt ready to take a deeper dive into the person she had become, to understand the journey she had walked and to embrace the future that awaited her. Her thoughts drifted to her mother's message from the day before. It had meant more to her than she could express. Her mother's support, tentative as it was, felt like the first true sense of belonging she had felt in years. But with that, came the weight of responsibility. Now that she had opened that door, there was no turning back.

Titi had always believed that if she could make it through the

CHAPTER 7

challenges of growing up in Nigeria, surrounded by societal expectations and cultural traditions, then she could face anything. But the battle she had fought for so long wasn't just with the world—it was with herself. It was the battle of owning her truth, of being authentic when so many tried to convince her that she didn't belong. And now that she had finally embraced that truth, she knew the journey ahead wouldn't be easy.

Her phone buzzed, breaking her from her thoughts. It was a message from Chika: *"You okay? Want to talk today? I'm free this afternoon."*

Titi smiled softly as she read the message. Chika had always been there for her, a constant source of support. She knew that whenever she needed to process her feelings, Chika would be there to listen. Titi had spent so much time keeping her thoughts bottled up, hiding her true self, but with Chika, she felt safe. She had built a friendship founded on trust, and it was that friendship that helped her see things in a clearer light.

Titi quickly typed back: *"I'm doing well. I think I might need to talk. Let's meet up later. I'll call you."*

She stood in front of the mirror again, taking in her reflection. She had come a long way since those early days, hiding behind layers of fear and uncertainty. Now, she looked at herself with a new sense of pride. Her confidence wasn't perfect, but it was real. She was learning to love who she was, inside and out.

As the day wore on, Titi felt her mind buzzing with thoughts of the future. She had started to make small changes in her life, from the way she interacted with people to the way she approached her work. She had been so focused on external validation for so long, seeking approval from others to define her worth. But now, she was focused on internal growth. She was no longer seeking permission to be who she was. The journey of self-acceptance was messy, but it was necessary.

Later that afternoon, Titi and Chika met at their favorite café in Victoria Island, a quiet spot they had frequented for years. It was a place that felt like home to them, with its rustic décor, quiet ambiance, and the comforting aroma of freshly brewed coffee. They sat down at their usual spot by the window, where they could people-watch and lose themselves in conversation.

"Okay, spill," Chika said, her eyes narrowing with curiosity as she leaned in. "What's been going on with you? You've been quiet lately."

Titi chuckled softly, taking a sip of her coffee before answering. "It's been a lot. I've been thinking a lot about what's next. My mom's message yesterday... I didn't expect it. She's trying, Chika. I can't believe she's actually trying."

Chika raised an eyebrow, a playful smirk appearing on her face. "Trying? So, you're telling me the woman who gave birth to you and has always been a little... well, extra, is finally starting to come around?"

Titi laughed. "Yeah, I guess so. It feels surreal. For so long, I thought it was impossible. I thought I'd never have her approval or support. But now... now, it feels like a new chapter is opening.

CHAPTER 7

And I don't know how to navigate it."

Chika took a deep breath, nodding in understanding. "That's a big deal. I know how much you've struggled with this. And I know how much it means to you to have her finally see you for who you really are. But you're right—it's a new chapter. And with that comes a whole new set of questions."

Titi nodded, her eyes clouding with uncertainty. "Exactly. I've spent so much time building walls, hiding, protecting myself. Now that those walls are coming down, I'm afraid of what might come next. What if things change again? What if she withdraws her support? What if I can't live up to the expectations she has for me?"

Chika reached across the table, placing her hand on Titi's. "First of all, you're not alone in this. You've got people who care about you, who will stand by you. Second, you don't have to live up to anyone's expectations but your own. You're already doing the hardest part, which is being honest with yourself. That's where the real growth happens."

Titi smiled, feeling a sense of relief wash over her. Chika always had a way of cutting through her doubts, reminding her of her strength. The truth was, Titi had been so focused on others' opinions for so long that she had lost sight of her own desires and dreams. She was so afraid of letting people down that she had forgotten to ask herself what she wanted out of life.

"You're right," Titi said softly, her voice steady. "I've been so focused on making everyone else happy that I've neglected myself. I need to take a step back and ask myself: What do I want? What's important to me?"

Chika grinned, her eyes sparkling with mischief. "Look at you, getting all deep and introspective. I love it."

Titi rolled her eyes, but she couldn't suppress the smile that tugged at her lips. "It's the truth, though. I've spent so much time living for other people. It's exhausting. I think I need to spend more time focusing on myself, on what makes me happy, what makes me feel fulfilled."

Chika's smile softened, her expression turning sincere. "I'm proud of you, Titi. I really am. It's not easy to take that step. You've always been strong, but now you're learning to be strong for yourself, not for anyone else."

Titi looked down at her hands, the weight of Chika's words sinking in. "I've spent so much time convincing myself that I needed to be perfect, that I needed to have it all figured out. But the truth is, I don't. And that's okay."

For a moment, the two women sat in silence, allowing the peace of the moment to settle around them. It was as if the noise of the world had faded, leaving only the connection between them.

"I think I'm ready," Titi said finally, her voice steady with resolve. "Ready to step into the next phase of my life. Ready to face whatever comes next, even if it's uncertain."

Chika smiled, her eyes filled with pride. "I knew you'd get here.

CHAPTER 7

You've always had it in you."

As they finished their coffee and prepared to leave, Titi felt lighter than she had in weeks. There was still uncertainty in her heart, still questions that lingered. But for the first time, she was beginning to trust herself. She wasn't afraid of what the future held. She was ready to face it head-on, with all the strength she had cultivated over the years.

And as she stepped into the bright Lagos sunlight, she felt a sense of hope stir within her. The world was wide open, and she was finally ready to walk through it as her true self. The journey was far from over, but for the first time, she was excited for what lay ahead.

Chapter 8

The evening breeze swept through the city, carrying with it a hint of the coming night. Lagos was vibrant as ever, its streets lined with the cacophony of honking horns, chattering pedestrians, and the unrelenting hum of city life. The noise, once overwhelming to Titi, now felt strangely comforting. It reminded her that, despite everything, the world was still moving, still progressing. And for the first time in years, she felt like she was too.

Titi's thoughts were on the conversation she had with Chika earlier. She had never considered how much power there was in simply acknowledging one's own feelings, in simply admitting to herself that she didn't have it all figured out. The pressure to be perfect, to have all the answers, had been suffocating. But Chika had helped her realize that it was okay not to know everything, that it was okay to take things one step at a time. It was a relief, a heavy weight lifting off her chest.

Still, as much as Titi had come to terms with her past and her

CHAPTER 8

identity, the uncertainty of what was to come lingered in the back of her mind. What did the future hold? What would her next steps be? She had started to carve out a space for herself in the world, but the journey was far from over. Every day brought new challenges, new questions. She had learned to embrace that uncertainty, but it didn't make it any less daunting.

The sound of her phone ringing brought her back to the present. The name on the screen made her pause for a moment: it was her mother. The last time they spoke, it had been an emotional conversation, one that left Titi feeling a mix of hope and fear. Her mother had expressed support, but also concerns, and though Titi understood her mother's worries, she couldn't help but feel the weight of the conversation. It was like a new chapter was beginning, but it was still too early to tell how the story would unfold.

Titi swiped to answer the call, taking a deep breath before she spoke.

"Hello, Mom," she said, trying to sound casual, though her heart was racing.

"Titi, my dear," her mother's voice came through warmly, though there was a hint of nervousness. "How are you? I've been thinking a lot about our conversation."

Titi's heart skipped a beat. "I'm doing well, Mom. Really, I am. It's been a lot to process, but I'm okay."

There was a brief silence on the other end of the line before her mother responded. "I've been praying, Titi. And I've been reflecting on everything we discussed. I want you to know that I'm here for you, even if I don't always know how to show it. This isn't easy for me, but I'm trying. I'm trying to understand."

Titi closed her eyes, feeling a mix of emotions. "Thank you, Mom. I know it's not easy. But I appreciate that you're trying. It means more to me than you know."

Her mother let out a soft sigh. "I know. And I want you to know that I love you. That will never change. I just... I need time. Time to adjust. But I'll get there, I promise."

Titi's chest tightened as she fought to hold back tears. "I know, Mom. I know. I'm not going anywhere."

After a few more minutes of conversation, the call ended, and Titi sat in silence, letting her mother's words wash over her. There was something undeniably reassuring about hearing her mother's voice, about knowing that, despite everything, she was still there. But even as she felt comforted, the truth was that the road ahead would be long. It wasn't just about navigating her relationship with her mother—it was about navigating her entire life, her place in the world, and her place within her own community.

The weight of it all pressed down on her, but she knew there was no turning back. She had already started this journey, and she wasn't going to let fear hold her back anymore.

Titi's phone buzzed again, this time with a message from Chika.

CHAPTER 8

"Let's meet up tomorrow. I have some news. I think you'll like it."

Titi smiled to herself. Chika had always been full of surprises. They had been friends for so long, and she could always count on Chika to lighten her mood, to offer support, or to simply be there when she needed someone to talk to. No matter what happened, Titi knew that Chika would always be her rock.

She responded quickly: *"I'll be there. Can't wait to hear what you have to say."*

The next day came faster than expected. Titi met Chika at the café, the place where they had shared countless conversations and secrets over the years. It was their safe space, a place where they could be their true selves without fear of judgment. Today, however, Titi was more anxious than usual. She had no idea what Chika had to share, but the anticipation was almost unbearable.

"Hey, you're here!" Chika greeted her with a smile, her eyes sparkling with excitement. "I've got something amazing to tell you."

Titi took a seat, trying to match Chika's enthusiasm, though she couldn't hide her nerves. "What's going on? You've got me all curious now."

Chika grinned, her excitement practically radiating from her. "Okay, okay, I'll spill. So, I've been working on something big. You know how we've always talked about doing something together? Something that would make a real impact? Well, I've been putting it into motion."

Titi's eyebrows furrowed. "What are you talking about?"

Chika leaned in closer, her voice dropping to a whisper as if she were revealing a secret. "I've been in talks with some people. People who want to help us create a platform for trans voices. A platform where people like us can share our stories, our experiences, and connect with others who understand. It's still in the early stages, but we've got a team. And I want you to be a part of it."

Titi's heart skipped a beat. "Wait, what? Are you serious? You're telling me that this is actually happening?"

Chika nodded eagerly. "Yes, it's real! We're going to create a space for trans people to share their truth. No filters, no shame. Just raw, authentic voices. And I want you to be there with me every step of the way."

Titi was stunned. The idea of a platform for trans voices, a space where they could be heard, felt like a dream come true. It was everything she had ever wanted—a place where she could finally share her story, where others could share theirs, and where they could be seen and celebrated for who they truly were.

For a moment, she couldn't speak. The weight of the opportunity settled in her chest, and she had to fight back the tears that threatened to fall. "Chika, this is... this is everything. You have no idea how much this means to me. To us."

CHAPTER 8

Chika's smile softened, her eyes filled with compassion. "I know, Titi. That's why I'm doing it. For all of us. We've spent so long hiding, so long living in the shadows. It's time for us to step into the light. And I want you by my side as we do it."

Titi took a deep breath, trying to steady herself. "I'm in. I'll do whatever it takes. I'm ready for this."

Chika's eyes gleamed with pride. "I knew you'd say that. Together, we're going to make something amazing happen."

As the two of them sat there, talking about the future and the possibilities that lay ahead, Titi felt a sense of clarity settle over her. This was the next step in her journey. This was her chance to create something meaningful, to help others like her find their voice and their place in the world. It wasn't going to be easy, but she was ready for the challenge.

For the first time in a long time, Titi felt like she was truly home. She was no longer just surviving; she was thriving, and with Chika by her side, she knew they could change the world. One story at a time.

Chapter 9

The sun had barely begun to dip beneath the horizon, casting long shadows over the busy streets of Lagos, when Titi arrived at the venue. The soft glow of twilight made the city feel almost magical, its usual hustle and bustle muted by the gentle evening breeze. Titi had always loved the energy of Lagos, the way it seemed to be constantly moving, constantly evolving. But tonight felt different. There was something in the air, something electric, like a moment of destiny was finally about to unfold.

She stood outside the building for a moment, looking up at its sleek modern façade, trying to calm the fluttering in her chest. This was the night. The night they would launch their platform. The platform that had been a dream for so long, one that had finally turned into a reality. She could feel the weight of it, the significance of what they were about to do. This wasn't just a website or an event—it was a movement. It was a declaration that their voices, their stories, mattered.

CHAPTER 9

Chika had been instrumental in making this happen. She had been relentless in her pursuit of this dream, using her connections, her drive, her unwavering belief that they could create something extraordinary. And now, it was all coming together. They had a team, they had a vision, and most importantly, they had a platform that was about to launch into the world, ready to make a difference.

Titi took a deep breath, steeling herself for what lay ahead. This was her moment too. She had spent years running from the spotlight, avoiding attention, keeping her story hidden in the shadows. But now, she was stepping into the light. It wasn't going to be easy, but she knew it was necessary. For herself, for Chika, and for everyone who would come after them.

As she entered the building, the buzz of excitement hit her like a wave. People were everywhere, setting up last-minute details, chatting with one another, their faces lit up with anticipation. There was a sense of camaraderie in the air, a shared excitement that seemed to fill every corner of the room. Titi's heart swelled as she took in the sight. This was what they had worked for. This was what they had dreamed of.

"Hey! You made it!" Chika's voice cut through the crowd, and Titi turned to see her friend pushing her way toward her with a big grin on her face. Chika's energy was infectious, and in an instant, Titi felt her nerves start to dissipate.

"I wouldn't miss it for the world," Titi said, smiling as she hugged Chika tightly. "This is incredible, Chika. I can't believe it's actually happening."

"I know!" Chika laughed, her eyes sparkling. "It feels surreal, doesn't it? But it's real. It's all real. And we're about to change the game, Titi."

Titi nodded, her heart swelling with pride. She had never felt so alive, so connected to something bigger than herself. This wasn't just about launching a platform—it was about creating a space where trans people could come together, share their stories, and find strength in each other. It was about giving a voice to those who had been silenced for too long, and showing the world that they mattered.

As the evening progressed, the venue filled with more and more people—activists, supporters, and members of the media. Titi moved through the crowd, meeting people who had come to show their support, to be a part of this historic moment. She felt a sense of pride that was both humbling and exhilarating. There were so many different faces, so many different stories in the room, all united by a common cause.

Eventually, the time came for the launch. Titi and Chika stood together on stage, the lights shining brightly down on them. Titi's heart raced as she looked out over the crowd. The room fell silent, all eyes on them. This was it. This was the moment that would define their journey.

"Good evening, everyone," Chika began, her voice strong and steady. "Thank you all for being here tonight. This is a night that marks the beginning of something incredibly special. We're here to launch something that we believe will make a real difference in the lives of trans people everywhere. But more

CHAPTER 9

than that, we're here to show the world that our stories, our voices, matter."

Titi stepped forward, her voice trembling slightly but gaining strength with each word. "We've all had to fight for our place in this world, to carve out a space where we can be seen, heard, and accepted for who we truly are. This platform is not just about us—it's about everyone who has ever felt invisible, unheard, or unloved. It's about creating a space where we can be ourselves, without fear, without shame."

There was a brief pause as Titi took a deep breath, gathering her thoughts. "This is the beginning of a revolution. A revolution of love, of acceptance, and of strength. Together, we will make sure our voices are heard. We will tell our stories, and in doing so, we will inspire others to do the same."

The room erupted in applause, and Titi felt a surge of emotion rise up within her. She had spoken from the heart, and the response was overwhelming. She looked over at Chika, who was beaming with pride, and for a moment, they shared a quiet moment of triumph. They had done it. They had built something that would change lives.

After the speech, the crowd began to mingle, and Titi found herself caught up in conversations with strangers and supporters. It felt like the world was finally waking up to the truth of their existence, and she was no longer afraid to be a part of that truth.

But as the night wore on, and the crowds began to thin, Titi's mind wandered back to the one question that had been lingering at the back of her mind for weeks: what now? What came after the launch? They had created something incredible, but the work wasn't over. In fact, it had only just begun. The platform was live, the world was watching, and now it was time to see how it would evolve.

Later that evening, as Titi sat with Chika in the quiet of the venue, the two of them shared a moment of reflection.

"This is just the beginning, isn't it?" Titi asked, her voice soft but filled with determination.

Chika nodded, her expression serious. "Yes, this is only the beginning. We've set the stage, but now we need to build on it. We need to keep pushing forward, to make sure our voices are heard loud and clear. We have a responsibility to our community, and we can't back down now."

Titi felt the weight of those words, but she also felt something else—a sense of purpose. She had never felt more certain of who she was, of what she wanted to do with her life. This platform was more than just a project. It was a mission. A mission to change the world, one story at a time.

"We will," Titi said, her voice steady now. "We will keep pushing forward. We'll make sure that this platform becomes everything we've dreamed of—and more."

As the last few people trickled out of the venue, Titi and Chika stood together, taking in the quiet that had settled over the space. It was a moment of peace, of reflection. But it was also a

CHAPTER 9

moment of anticipation. They had started something big, and the road ahead was full of possibility.

In the weeks that followed, the platform began to gain traction. Trans people from all over the world began to share their stories, their experiences, and their struggles. The platform became a space of healing and empowerment, a place where individuals could come together and find support in one another. The world began to take notice, and with every story shared, Titi felt a sense of purpose grow stronger within her. This was what she was meant to do. This was her calling.

And with Chika by her side, she knew that there was nothing they couldn't accomplish. Together, they would continue to change the world, one story at a time.

Chapter 10

The soft hum of the city echoed in the distance, and Titi sat at her desk, the glow of her laptop screen casting a quiet light on her face. She had always been a night owl, and tonight, as the clock ticked past midnight, she felt a sense of peace settling over her. The platform had grown beyond what she had ever imagined. What had started as a dream, a hope that she and Chika had nurtured together, had become something powerful, something that had touched so many lives.

As she looked back at the journey, it seemed almost surreal. The late nights spent coding and refining, the constant brainstorming sessions with Chika, the endless conversations about the future—everything had led to this. It had been difficult at times, filled with challenges that seemed insurmountable. But they had pushed through, driven by their shared vision of creating a space where trans voices could be heard, where people could find solace, strength, and validation. And now, the platform was flourishing, bringing together individuals from every corner of the world, united by their shared experiences and identities.

CHAPTER 10

Titi smiled to herself as she thought about how far they had come. When she first stepped into this journey, she had been unsure of herself, uncertain of her place in the world. But with each passing day, she had found her confidence, her voice. The platform had given her more than just a career—it had given her purpose. It had allowed her to reclaim her narrative, to share her story with the world, and to stand proudly in her truth.

But it wasn't just her story that was being told. It was the stories of countless others—people who had lived in the shadows, who had been silenced by society, who had been told that they didn't matter. Now, their voices were being amplified, their experiences shared, their struggles acknowledged. The platform had become a place of community, a sanctuary where people could come together and support each other, lifting one another up in a world that often felt so isolating.

Titi's thoughts were interrupted by the sound of her phone buzzing on the desk. She picked it up and saw Chika's name flashing across the screen. She smiled and answered the call.

"Hey, Chika. What's up?"

"Hey, Titi," Chika's voice crackled with excitement. "You won't believe this, but we've got another feature story lined up. It's a huge opportunity, and they want us to be the ones to write it!"

Titi's heart skipped a beat. "Really? That's amazing!"

"I know, right? The publisher reached out to us because they've been following the platform, and they want us to cover the impact of trans visibility in the media. It's a big deal, Titi. This could be the breakthrough we've been waiting for."

Titi leaned back in her chair, her mind racing with possibilities. This was the kind of opportunity they had dreamed about—the kind that could elevate the platform to new heights, bringing their message to an even wider audience. She could already see the impact it could have, the doors it could open.

"That's incredible, Chika. I'm so proud of us," Titi said, her voice filled with pride. "We've worked so hard to get to this point, and now the world is starting to take notice."

Chika's laughter echoed through the phone. "We've only just begun, my friend. There's so much more ahead of us. But this is definitely a major milestone. We're making waves, Titi. We're really doing it."

Titi smiled to herself, feeling a rush of gratitude. She had been in this for the long haul, and now, it felt like everything was finally coming together. She thought back to all the moments when she had doubted herself, when she had wondered if this dream was even worth pursuing. But every step had been worth it. Every challenge had made them stronger, and every setback had been an opportunity to learn and grow.

She and Chika had been through so much together, and now they were standing at the precipice of something even greater. Titi knew that the road ahead would still have its share of obstacles, but she felt ready to face them. They were no longer just two people with a vision—they were a force to be reckoned with, and

CHAPTER 10

they had a platform that was poised to make a lasting impact.

As Titi sat back in her chair, her mind wandered back to the early days of their journey. It felt like a lifetime ago when they first began this project, unsure of where it would lead. But now, as she looked at the success they had achieved, she couldn't help but feel a sense of pride. They had created something beautiful, something that had the power to change lives. And they weren't done yet.

Titi's phone buzzed again, this time with a message. She glanced at it and saw that it was from one of their community members, someone who had been active on the platform since the beginning. The message was simple but powerful: "Thank you for creating this space. It has saved my life."

Titi's heart swelled as she read the words. This was why they did it. This was why they had poured their hearts and souls into the platform—to help people like this, to provide a space where they could be seen, heard, and loved for who they truly were. In that moment, Titi realized that their work was far from over. There were still so many people out there who needed them, who needed to find this community, this sense of belonging.

She thought of the future—of the ways they could continue to expand their reach, of the stories they still needed to tell, of the people they still needed to help. The platform had grown beyond what they had ever imagined, but it was only the beginning. Titi felt a fire ignite within her. There was so much more to do, so much more to give. And she was ready.

A knock on the door interrupted her thoughts. It was Chika, her face beaming with excitement as she stepped into the room. "Are you ready for this next chapter?" Chika asked, her voice full of energy.

Titi stood up and smiled. "I'm more than ready, Chika. Let's make the most of this. Let's change the world."

Together, they stood at the threshold of something incredible. They had built something that had already made a difference in so many lives, but there was still so much more to be done. The world was waiting, and they were ready to step into it, to take their place at the forefront of the fight for trans rights and visibility.

As they stood there, looking out at the future, Titi felt a deep sense of fulfillment. They had come a long way, but the journey was far from over. With Chika by her side, she knew that they could achieve anything. And as the world continued to evolve, so too would their platform—growing, expanding, and making a difference for generations to come.

Titi took a deep breath, her heart filled with hope. This was just the beginning.